Animal Coverings

By Connor Stratton

level
2
little blue
readers

www.littlebluehousebooks.com

Little Blue House is distributed by North Star Editions:
sales@northstareditions.com | 888-417-0195

Produced for Little Blue House by Red Line Editorial.

Photographs ©: Shutterstock Images, cover, 4 (top), 4 (bottom), 15, 21 (bottom), 24 (top left); iStockphoto, 7 (top), 7 (bottom), 8–9, 11 (top), 11 (bottom), 12, 16–17, 18, 21 (top), 23 (top), 23 (bottom), 24 (top right), 24 (bottom left), 24 (bottom right)

Library of Congress Control Number: 2020900788

ISBN
978-1-64619-173-4 (hardcover)
978-1-64619-207-6 (paperback)
978-1-64619-275-5 (ebook pdf)
978-1-64619-241-0 (hosted ebook)

Printed in the United States of America
Mankato, MN
082020

About the Author

Connor Stratton enjoys spotting new animals and writing books for children. He lives in Minnesota.

Table of Contents

Many Coverings

All animals have coverings.
Some coverings are hard,
and others are soft.

Shells cover

some animals.

Snails have shells.

Turtles have shells too.

Skeletons cover some animals.

They cover scorpions.

They keep these animals safe.

scorpion

skeleton

Scales cover

some animals.

Snakes have scales.

Fish have scales too.

Skin and Hair

Some animals

have skin and hair.

Hippos have thick skin.

They have some hair.

Foxes have a lot of hair.

It covers their skin.

Thick hair is called fur.

fox

fur

Porcupines have spines.

Spines are sharp hairs.

Feathers

Birds have feathers.
A peacock has many
bright green feathers.

Some feathers are brown, and others are white. Some feathers are red, and others are green.

Some feathers are shiny.

Other feathers look

like wood.

23

Glossary

fox

peacock

hippo

scorpion

Index